THE WORLD'S DIRTIEST MACHINES

Thi

The
a fu

Jennifer Blizin Gillis

Raintree

www.raintreepublishers.co.uk
Visit our website to find out more information about Raintree books.

To order:
☎ Phone 0845 6044371
📄 Fax +44 (0) 1865 312263
🖳 Email myorders@raintreepublishers.co.uk

Customers from outside the UK please telephone +44 1865 312262

Raintree is an imprint of Capstone Global Library Limited, a company incorporated in England and Wales having its registered office at 7 Pilgrim Street, London, EC4V 6LB – Registered company number: 6695582

Text © Capstone Global Library Limited 2011
First published in hardback in 2011
The moral rights of the proprietor have been asserted.

Edited by Nancy Dickmann and Megan Cotugno
Designed by Jo Hinton-Malivoire
Picture research by Tracy Cummins
Originated by Capstone Global Library
Printed and bound in China by CTPS

ISBN 978 1 406216 88 2 (hardback)
15 14 13 12 11
10 9 8 7 6 5 4 3 2 1

ISBN 978 1 406219 75 3 (paperback)
16 15 14 13 12
10 9 8 7 6 5 4 3 2 1

British Library Cataloguing in Publication Data
Gillis, Jennifer Blizin, 1950-
The world's dirtiest machines. -- (Extreme machines)
628-dc22
A full catalogue record for this book is available from the British Library.

Acknowledgments
We would like to thank the following for permission to reproduce photographs: Alamy p. **21** (Peter Titmuss); Corbis pp. **10** (© Gerd Ludwig), **12** (© Steve Crisp/Reuters), **13** (© Koen van Weel /Reuters), **14** (© Joel W. Rogers), **15** (© Alan Schein Photography), **17** (© Ashley Cooper), **24** (© Al Satterwhite/Transtock), **27** (© Richard Hamilton Smith); Getty Images pp. **4** (WIN-Initiative), **18** (Paul Chesley), **20** (Ken Welsh), **25** (AFP/FAYEZ NURELDINE); istockphoto p. **7** (© Mike Clarke); Photolibrary pp. **6** (Andreas Schlegel), **11** (Imagesource Imagesource); Shutterstock pp. **5** (© Nethunter), **8** (© SergioZ), **9** (© SergioZ), **16** (© Sergios), **19** (© Zacarias Pereira da Mata), **22** (© Liz Van Steenburgh), **23** (© tomazzi), **26** (© Dmitry Naumov).

Cover photograph of full track loader reproduced with permission of Corbis (© Jim Zuckerman).

Some words are shown in bold, **like this**. You can find out what they mean by looking in the glossary.

Contents

Doing dirty work

All over the world, there are dirty jobs to do. Dirty machines help with this dirty work. Dirty machines dig, suck, smash, crush, and dump.

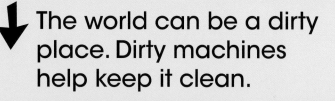

The world can be a dirty place. Dirty machines help keep it clean.

5

Rubbish removers

Bin lorries pick up solid waste. Some have **hydraulic** arms that pick up rubbish bins. Workers throw rubbish into the back of other lorries. A huge blade smashes and crushes the rubbish so the lorry can hold more.

hydraulic arm

blade

EXTREME FACT
A full lorry holds up to 13 tonnes of waste. That is a lot of rubbish!

Waste smashers

Bin lorries dump their loads in **landfill sites.** Landfill **compactors** roll over the mountains of rubbish. They have spiked metal wheels. Their blades push and crush the rubbish to make room for more.

blade

spikes

EXTREME FACT
The Caterpillar 836H landfill compactor weighs almost 54,431 kilograms. That's as much as six school buses!

Dirty tractors

Tractors on a farm need to get dirty. Some have **mulchers** attached that break up the dirt. This makes it easier to plant seeds.

Tractors do other jobs too. When the land is ready, they plant the seeds. Then they water them. These can be dirty jobs!

Filthy ships

Dredgers are boats that pull up sand, dirt, and rocks from underwater. Long hoses reach deep down. They suck up the sand at the bottom of rivers and seas. Some dredgers pump sand out on to the shore.

A hose under this ship is sucking up sand.

EXTREME FACT
The largest dredgers can hold enough sand to fill more than 10,000 sandpits!

Barges are open ships shaped like rectangles. They carry rubbish and other dirty loads. Some bin lorries dump their loads into barges. The barges carry the rubbish to **landfill sites.**

coal

scrap metal

↑ Nets keep the rubbish from blowing into the water.

15

Dirty excavators

Excavators are powerful diggers. They have a long arm called a boom. A bucket on the end scoops up heavy loads. Excavators can pick up trees or knock down buildings. An attachment called a thumb pinches and pulls.

boom

bucket

thumb

17

Dumper trucks

Dumper trucks carry away dirt and other rubbish. Other machines fill the dumper truck. The loads can weigh hundreds of tonnes. Dumper trucks have extra wheels at the back to carry these heavy loads.

double wheels

drop box

A **hydraulic system** uses oil to push up one end of the drop box. This tips the box, so that the load slides out of the back.

Off-road dumpers

In mines and **quarries,** dumper trucks go up and down steep hills. The cab and truck bed of **articulated dumper trucks** move separately. This stops the truck from tipping over.

bed

cab

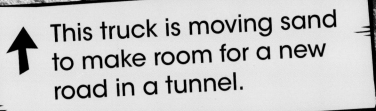

This truck is moving sand to make room for a new road in a tunnel.

Dirty 'dozers

What can clean up tonnes of mud? Bulldozers! Some bulldozers have giant tyres that help them drive through sand or mud. Bulldozers use different blades to push heavy loads. A u-blade is the most common.

u-blade

tracks

Most of these big machines move on tracks.

Fun and dirty

Huge engines roar. At a mud drag race, cars and trucks zoom down a short, flat, muddy track. As the racing cars take off, mud sprays everywhere.

There are many kinds of mud racing vehicles. People make changes to their cars and trucks so they can go faster in mud races.

All-terrain vehicles (ATVs) race in mud, too. In Championship Mud Racing, riders race their ATVs around an oval track where the mud can be over a metre deep!

EXTREME FACT

The dirtiest machines may be ATV mud boggers. Their extra large tyres keep them driving through mud pits. Long tubes called snorkels let air into their engines but keep mud out.

Test yourself!

Match each sentence with the correct vehicle.

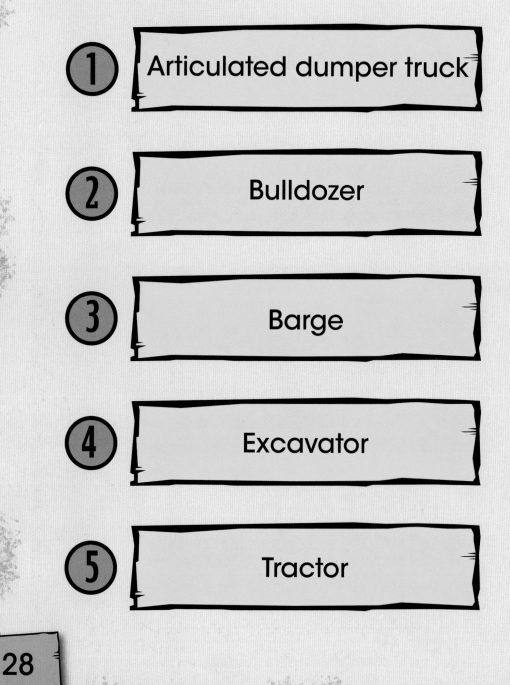

1. Articulated dumper truck

2. Bulldozer

3. Barge

4. Excavator

5. Tractor

This dirty machine breaks up dirt on a farm.

The long arm on this dirty machine is called a boom.

This kind of dirty truck can climb steep hills in mines or quarries.

These dirty machines have blades that can scrape up mud.

Flat-bottomed boats like these carry dirty loads.

Glossary

articulated dumper truck vehicle built with sections that can move by themselves

compactor machine that can crush things to save space

dredger machine that takes sand, soil, and rocks from underwater

excavator large machine used for digging and pulling

hydraulic moved by the power of liquid, such as water or oil, being forced through a narrow tube

landfill site large piece of land where rubbish is buried in between layers of soil

mulcher machine that breaks up soil on farms

quarry open pit where rock or stone is dug out by machine

Find out more

Books

Diggers and Dumpers, Jayne Parsons (Dorling Kindersley, 2005)

Fifty Trucks to Spot, Felicity Parker (Usborne, 2009)

Off-road Racing, Lee-Anne Spalding (Rourke, 2009)

Websites

Caterpillar trucks
http://www.cat.com/equipment
Pictures and descriptions of all of the heavy equipment made by Caterpillar, including rubbish compactors, dumper trucks, excavators, and more.

Mud racers
http://www.mudracersassociation.com
Information about all kinds of muddy off-road races and vehicles, plus detailed action photos.

More extreme machines
http://www.worsleyschool.net/science/files/extreme/machines.html
Pictures and descriptions of some of the biggest construction vehicles on Earth.

Find out

What is a knuckleboom loader?

Index